How to Promote Your Children's Book

HOW TO PROMOTE YOUR CHILDREN'S BOOK

Series "How to Promote"
By: D.K. Hawkins
Version 1.1 ~November 2022
Published by D.K. Hawkins at KDP
Copyright ©2022 by D.K. Hawkins. All rights reserved.

No part of this publication may be reproduced, distributed, or transmitted in any form or by any means including photocopying, recording, or other electronic or mechanical methods or by any information storage or retrieval system without the prior written permission of the publishers, except in the case of very brief quotations embodied in critical reviews and certain other noncommercial uses permitted by copyright law.

All rights reserved, including the right of reproduction in whole or in part in any form.

All information in this book has been carefully researched and checked for factual accuracy. However, the author and publisher make no warranty, express or implied, that the information contained herein is appropriate for every individual, situation, or purpose and assume no responsibility for errors or omissions.

The reader assumes the risk and full responsibility for all actions. The author will not be held responsible for any loss or damage, whether consequential, incidental, special or otherwise, that may result from the information presented in this book.

All images are free for use or purchased from stock photo sites or royalty-free for commercial use. I have relied on my own observations as well as many different sources for this book, and I have done my best to check facts and give credit where it is due. In the event that any material is used without proper permission, please contact me so that the oversight can be corrected.

The information provided in this book is for informational purposes only and is not intended to be a source of advice or credit analysis with respect to the material presented. The information and/or documents contained in this book do not constitute legal or financial advice and should never be used without first consulting with a financial professional to determine what may be best for your individual needs.

The publisher and the author do not make any guarantee or other promise as to any results that may be obtained from using the content of this book. You should never make any investment decision without first consulting with your own financial advisor and conducting your own research and due diligence. To the maximum extent permitted by law, the publisher and the author disclaim any and all liability in the event any information, commentary, analysis, opinions, advice, and/or recommendations contained in this book prove to be inaccurate, incomplete, or unreliable or result in any investment or other losses.

Content contained or made available through this book is not intended to and does not constitute legal advice or investment advice, and no attorney-client relationship is formed. The publisher and the author are providing this book and its contents on an "as is" basis. Your use of the information in this book is at your own risk.

TABLE OF CONTENTS.

How to Promote Your Children's Book 0

TABLE OF CONTENTS. 3

INTRODUCTION 5

CHAPTER 1: WRITING CHILDREN'S BOOKS. 9

CHAPTER 2: EXCELLENT PROMOTIONAL METHODS AFTER WRITING YOUR FIRST BOOK FOR YOUNG CHILDREN. 17

CHAPTER 3; INCREASE CHILDREN'S BOOK VISIBILITY THROUGH AUTHOR APPEARANCES. 22

CHAPTER 4: BOOK REVIEWS AS YOUR MOST EFFECTIVE PROMOTIONAL TOOL. 26

CHAPTER 5: USING IMAGES OF YOUR BOOK FOR PROMOTION. 32

CHAPTER 6: HOW TO PROMOTE YOUR CHILDREN'S EBOOK THROUGH SPEAKING ENGAGEMENTS. 39

CHAPTER 7: HOW TO CONSTRUCT YOUR AUTHOR PLATFORM TO IMPROVE CHILDREN'S BOOK PROMOTION. 44

CHAPTER 8: WHY SOME AUTHORS NEVER SUCCEED AS CHILDREN'S AUTHORS. 52

CHAPTER 9: SUBMISSIONS TO CONTRACT TO BOOK MARKETING TO WRITING PROFESSION. 58

CHAPTER 10: ONLINE BOOK MARKETING. 64

CHAPTER 11; ENSURE YOU HAVE A REMARKABLE BOOK COVER. 69

CHAPTER 12: SUGGESTIONS FOR FINDING CHILDREN'S BOOK PUBLISHERS. 73

CHAPTER 13: WRITING FOR CHILDREN AND WINNING OVER PARENTS. 77

CHAPTER 14; BOOSTING THE VISIBILITY OF YOUR SELF-PUBLISHED CHILDREN'S BOOK. 81

CHAPTER 15: MAKING YOUR CHILDREN'S BOOK A BESTSELLER. 85

CHAPTER 16: UTILIZING CUSTOM-MADE BOBBLE HEADS FOR PROMOTION. 90

CHAPTER 17: CONSIDERATIONS TO MAKE BEFORE PUBLISHING A CHILDREN'S EBOOK 94

CHAPTER 18; BOOK MARKETING TIPS THAT WILL HELP YOU SELL MORE COPIES. 98

CHAPTER 19: BOOK PROMOTION MISTAKES TO AVOID. 102

CHAPTER 20: PROMOTE YOUR BOOK IN YOUR NEIGHBORHOOD. 109

CONCLUSION. 113

INTRODUCTION.

For many writers and authors, writing and publishing a children's book is a lifelong ambition. Unfortunately, most excellent writers do not know or understand the measures to take to begin the process of becoming known and published, making it difficult for them to accomplish their dream.

Do you need an agency, an illustrator, an assistant, a consultant, or book marketing services?

Do you know which Children's Publishing Houses you should send your work to first for the greatest profit and the best acceptance rate?

Have you determined the type of Children's Book you intend to write?

The Children's Book Publishing industry can be difficult to navigate for the uninformed but is straightforward for those with knowledge. Writing and introducing one's work to the market is a piece of cake for those with experience.

You may have the next best-selling children's book, but if you don't know how to expose it to the market, you'll keep hitting walls, much like most struggling children's authors who, tragically, don't make it past the early phase of the publishing process.

Finding a trustworthy individual to explain how the entire industry operates will be difficult. Consultants can be costly and seasoned, and well-known Children's Book Publishers rarely divulge their trade secrets to other children's book publishers. After all, why would they put themselves in a situation where they could lose their book's fame and income?

Yes, hundreds of publications on how to write, promote and publish a children's book, but the majority do not make the publishing process simple to comprehend. If you follow most Children's Book Publishing courses, you will discover that they are inefficient and could cost you a lot of time.

A formula for auto-pilot that no other Children's Book Publishing manual can match. No author desires to comb through hundreds of pages of Children's Book Publishing strategies and concepts. To be successful in this children's book industry, you must get to the point and get things done.

Education is essential whether you want to write, sell, advertise or publish a Children's Book, whether a picture book or a standard book. Hundreds of thousands of writers go undetected every year, and many priceless Children's Books are shelved or never sold to a publishing house due to a lack of business expertise. Don't be in this position!

You must learn how to target your age group, generate tale ideas, develop your characters, design a story arc, introduce your characters with descriptions of their physical and personality features, establish a problem or conflict, and set the stage for the climax.

Character development, storylines, conflict and resolution, and marketing and publication skills are required to be a successful children's author. This

GUIDE explores effective strategies for promoting children's books and becoming successful authors.

Let's get started.

CHAPTER 1: WRITING CHILDREN'S BOOKS.

As adults, we all recall the books we read avidly as children. I remember the joy I felt every Friday when I rushed home from school, knowing that my grandmother would have the next Roald Dahl novel waiting for me. The Twits and The BFG are tales I will never forget. As I'm certain, they will be by many other 1980s children.

In light of this, it bothers me when people imply that creating a children's book is a simple alternative or a stepping stone to writing an adult novel. When producing a children's book, much consideration is required, especially considering how susceptible youngsters are to outside influences.

It is important to comprehend the impact that the book's writing and themes would have on the child. Writing a novel for children is more restricted than writing for adults.

The topic, terminology, and length must be carefully considered. A child is impressionable and will investigate the perspectives and ideas in books, which will invariably influence their own lives. The child's language and vocabulary will impact his or her intelligence and schooling. Thus, this must also be appropriately assessed.

For this reason, writing a children's book is extremely difficult and needs time-consuming research. So, if the topic, vocabulary, and length follow parental and educational guidelines, it is time to engage and connect with the intended audience: the child.

In certain circumstances, a youngster can be an adult's worst critic. With their naiveté, they are certain to exhibit sincerity and genuine feeling in the purest form when reading your work. They have not yet learned the ability to communicate constructive criticism politely; instead, they speak from the heart as they feel fit.

To enter the field of writing for children is often a ridiculed and intrusive endeavor. Therefore, you must conduct research first and foremost. Your book will be evaluated by the adults exploring child development through literature, including parents, teachers, the government, and publishers. Individual readers will evaluate your novel.

Only then can you unleash your creative writing talent. The world of children's book writing may be difficult, but it will be a fulfilling craft when you achieve it, and children all over the world will read and love your incredibly inventive book.

Writing a children's book needs a vivid imagination, inventiveness with words, and zeal. The most essential element is the capacity to perceive through the eyes of a youngster. Therefore, you must conduct a study beforehand.

Creating entertaining material for a youngster needs a novel and curious perspective on the world. For a child to be fully engaged, enthusiastic, and interested in your book, it must be relatable to him or her.

What are today's children interested in?

What are their likes and dislikes?

What words do they use to communicate with one another?

What books do they read?

What toys do they play with?

What songs do they like?

What clothes do they wear?

What magazines do they purchase?

What are they afraid of? And What excites them?

From this, you will be able to determine the type of writing that will effectively reach your target audience and make your book famous.

After exhaustively researching and investigating children's preferences, you can move on to the plot. This section needs the use of your talent, energy, and ingenuity.

This is the most crucial consideration. You must determine the type of book you wish to write, the issues you wish to explore, the messages you want to convey, and the desired outcome. Many authors favor developing their books through participatory workshops, and if it is a business concept, goods and sequels may follow.

Therefore, this will all need to be determined while creating the narrative. Ensure that your decision is consistent with the research you have conducted. Even include references to novels you enjoyed as a child and current literature. While writing your story, it is crucial to remember that children have a shorter attention span and less concentration than adults.

As a writer, it is essential to maintain literature as a current form of entertainment on par with Xbox and PlayStation. Therefore, a story must be basic and straightforward to capture their attention immediately. Finally, it should be relevant, amusing, and enjoyable.

The language and vocabulary used in children's literature are also essential for developing their intelligence and concentration. It is beneficial to increase vocabulary by reading, but if a youngster cannot read the words, they will lose interest and concentration. Avoiding complex phrases that a toddler cannot comprehend is advantageous.

According to research, a youngster does not value more than a few words per sentence. This is significant advice for a novice writer, as it is simple to risk embellishing and elaborating texts due to prior writing experience.

A book should inspire constructive intellectual, personal and emotional development; hence it should not contain slang, bad language, or inappropriate topics. The writing should be of the highest quality and standard appropriate for the age range, and it should inspire young readers to appreciate their language and desire to read more.

The themes you choose to incorporate into the narrative are crucial and quite diverse. A book can effectively encourage children to embrace and implement positive affirmations in their own life. As long as the tale has a happy ending, the book will positively affect a child's outlook on life. Too many negative influences are affecting their life as they get older.

A child will love their characters living happily ever after, encouraging them to confront their challenges with optimism. Characters should have positive attributes, such as courage, humor, and honesty, that children can emulate.

Literature is useful for inspiring positive, healthy children and providing them with escape and enjoyment. This, along with the abovementioned elements, is necessary for writing a successful children's book. As long as a bright, happy, and colorful world is established and the topics are meaningful to a youngster, I am confident it will be appreciated.

I enthusiastically encourage everyone reading this who believes they can write a children's book to do it. We need as many influential children's authors actively publishing to keep this form of inspiration and child development alive.

CHAPTER 2: EXCELLENT PROMOTIONAL METHODS AFTER WRITING YOUR FIRST BOOK FOR YOUNG CHILDREN.

Young children's books are one genre that e-publishing will never totally supplant. The kindle will never be able to compete with the tactile nature of popular children's books.

Most books contain thick, durable pages, materials in or on the pages, and pop-out images; some are waterproof. These books are very costly to produce, and the category is extremely competitive, so if you are a first-time author of books for very young children, you must always keep marketing in mind.

Utilize Tactile Brochures To Promote Your Books.

A sample of your writing is the most effective promotional tool for a book. You should be particularly inventive when producing brochures featuring a small excerpt of your work for distribution to publishers and readers.

If you network effectively, interesting brochures will aid in the promotion of your book. Since you are selling to parents of small children, your brochure should be truly impressive.

Experiment with the design of the brochure and ask a local or online printing business if they can add anything eye-catching, such as foil or a mirrored coating, to the page. If you select an example of writing that relates to this, children will enjoy the brochure when it is presented.

Stickers are always popular with children.

While bookmarks containing a sample of your writing would work well with an adult book, promoting a book for young children needs a bit more creativity. A printing business may assist you in designing bookmarks with stickers or stickers that may be inserted into books or pamphlets.

Stickers promoting your books will be more effective if they feature a striking design with your book's title and vivid graphics. Parents are more likely to assess favorably novels in which their children have demonstrated an interest.

Badges To Stand Out.

When visiting publishers or meeting with parents at conventions or book fairs, having button badges produced will be of great assistance. People will be enticed to explore your brochure by buttons depicting a character from your novel. There is a safety concern with providing buttons to young children. However, most parents will allow their children to wear a badge under supervision.

Removing the button before washing the garments may remind parents of your brochure. If children recall the button the following day, this will boost your likelihood of generating a sale.

You can lower the cost by purchasing blank buttons in bulk and finding a vendor to print you inexpensive stickers. Using the stickers to make your buttons will need some effort.

Colorful Leaflets.

Most young children cannot resist the opportunity to color. Thus, developing a flyer for your book with a colorable space is one of the most effective and cost-effective methods for promoting your book. The goal is to make the flyer's borders dynamic and snappy so that the center begs to be colored.

Captivate Publishers And Readers.

This is the most expensive option, but you'd be surprised at how inexpensive it can be to get large quantities of flat refrigerator magnets printed. A character from your first children's story can be printed on them. People are less hesitant to abandon a magnet; very often, they'll become a permanent feature on someone's fridge and children's occasional play object.

As with the badge idea, blank fridge magnets can be bulk-bought for a fraction of the cost of professionally produced ones. You can design your personalized magnets by ordering sheets of stickers. These won't survive as long, but they'll do for promotion.

CHAPTER 3; INCREASE CHILDREN'S BOOK VISIBILITY THROUGH AUTHOR APPEARANCES.

The author's engagement in a public speaking campaign is a proven technique to spread the news about their book. The novels of authors who pursue speaking engagements receive more notice. Some authors have single-handedly catapulted their works to bestseller status by continuously traveling and lecturing nationwide.

Even if an author cannot travel and talk often owing to other obligations, this part of book marketing should not be overlooked. Even a few speaking events will help authors build a dedicated readership and improve book sales.

Getting Going.

Local bookshops and libraries are excellent areas for authors to begin discussing the subject of their works. Many retailers (particularly Borders and Barnes & Noble) will conduct brief author seminars for their customers. Libraries also do this. After these events, authors who take advantage of these opportunities can increase their book sales by selling autographed copies of their works.

Nonfiction authors typically have a natural-speaking topic. However, authors of fiction and children's books can create speaking chances. During National Literacy Month, for instance, children's book authors can volunteer to read their works in a bookshop or library (September).

An author of young adult literature can volunteer to teach teens a short fiction writing course at a local library. Authors of mysteries can take advantage of Barnes & Noble's Mystery Month in October. These are but a handful of the many chances that authors can develop to organize speaking engagements to promote their novels.

While creating a speaking career takes time, public speaking can be profitable for authors who include it in their book marketing strategy. Initially, authors typically need to talk for free and leverage each speaking engagement to sell books. However, authors can charge for their services once they establish a speaking business.

If an author lacks public speaking experience or is afraid of speaking in front of a group, he or she might consider reading books on public speaking or enrolling in public speaking workshops.

Acquisition of Speaking Engagements.

Speaking engagements must be actively pursued and cultivated. Opportunities are only presented to authors who have developed the speaking aspect of their trade over time. Most new speakers will need to invest time in securing speaking engagements.

Many events include authors as keynote speakers. Authors can pursue speaking engagements by identifying events and groups that cater to their book's intended audience as potential speaking venues.

For instance, a book on safe dating practices for adolescents could lead to speaking engagements at middle and high schools and community and church youth organizations.

Once an event or group has been discovered as a suitable speaking location, the author will contact the event's or group's organizers and submit a profile, speaking topic, and synopsis for consideration.

How many books may be sold by public speaking? It depends on the occasion, the speaker, and the listener. Whether the number of book sales is three or three hundred, each speaking engagement is an opportunity for exposure. Also, publicity generates future book sales.

CHAPTER 4: BOOK REVIEWS AS YOUR MOST EFFECTIVE PROMOTIONAL TOOL.

Book reviews are an effective method of advertising your publication. Most readers rely on trustworthy reviews since professional reviewers are objective and respected by most readers. Finding decent reviewers is problematic for many authors, especially less experienced ones.

With over 500,000 new books being published annually, the demand for reviews has surged dramatically. Today, it is quite difficult to get a review from a widely recognized reviewer. To give you an idea of the whole issue, Publishers Weekly, the premier journal in the industry, examines only 5,000 books annually.

Midwest Book Reviews reviews around 490 books per month and is one of the nation's largest review organizations. Nonetheless, there is no cause to be irritated. There are many options for perceptive authors to compose insightful reviews.

How Can I Find a Reviewer?

There are many credible sources to which you might turn. Dan Poynter, a publishing expert of the highest caliber, provides you the opportunity to list your book for review in his digital newsletter titled "para publishing." Authors anxious to see their names in print will offer to review your book.

Poynter requests that reviewers who register on his website refrain from posting unpleasant comments. He clarifies that he is not requesting the reviewer to alter his or her views. He just begs that you say nothing if you cannot offer something positive.

Amazon's Top 1000 Reviewers are the largest collection of professional reviewers. Any review endorsed by this organization will be highly regarded and relied upon.

Enter "Amazon Top Reviewers" into your search engine to get a list of reviewers and their ranks. Do not expect a review from the top 50 or 100 websites. They are exceptionally busy and selective. If you have the time, kindly give it a shot. It's conceivable. I have personal experience with this.

It is essential to consider more than these reviewers. If you have authored a nonfiction book, send a request for a review to periodicals that cover the same subject. If successful, it will be viewed by readers of the journal who have already demonstrated an interest in this subject and have a high likelihood of purchasing.

Also, consult local newspapers. There are specific sections for business, seniors, food, travel, and real estate in the biggest daily. Send your request for review to the appropriate section's editor.

Sadly, many newspapers have eliminated their book review sections, though others still publish reviews on other pages. Be sure to contact the local weekly newspapers. They are well-read and constantly on the lookout for interesting stories about the achievements of local individuals.

Enter "Book Reviewers" on the Internet but screen your responses well. Be suspicious of bought reviews. They don't carry the same weight as unpaid employees. However, there are some valuable paid reviews. ForeWord Magazine has begun a paid scheme that will garner respect, much as Normal Goldman's paid evaluations of Bookpleasures.com.

Prepublication Evaluations.

Authors often miss a type of review that is of critical importance. Before a book is released, only the seven most significant magazines in our sector do reviews. People in the industry mostly view these reviews. A positive review on any of them will help assure substantial sales before your book is published.

The seven primary reviewers before publication are Editor's Weekly, New York Times, Library Journal, Kirkus Review, and ForeWordMagazine.

Book Review and Booklist (American Library Association)

If your book is appropriate for children or adolescents, include School Library Journal. Four months before publication, you must deliver galleys of your book enclosed in a cover (or a copy) to the reviewer. The cover must indicate

"Advanced Review Copy - Not Completely Edited." Even if you have a completed copy of the book, you should not submit it. This reviewer will only accept advanced copies (ARCs).

You may opt to hire a digital printer specializing in short runs and have bound copies created. However, these must also bear the ARC notification on the cover. You will inevitably need more copies than the ones you send to these reviewers.

You may wish to promote book clubs, distribute to additional reviewers, include an ARC with endorsement requests, and use your book for other promotional purposes.

Once the book has been published, it goes without saying that you will continue to solicit as many reviews as possible and ensure that a significant number of them are placed on Amazon.com, Barnes & Noble.com, Borders.com, and Books-a-Million.com. Do not overlook the many internet bookstores which are Amazon affiliates.

CHAPTER 5: USING IMAGES OF YOUR BOOK FOR PROMOTION.

Typically, books have at least two images: the cover art and the author's photograph. Other publications may have many black-and-white or color inside photographs, illustrations, maps, or other forms of graphics.

All these photographs can be used to market your book, even if customers purchase online and cannot examine a real copy before purchasing. Before your book is released or even set out, take the time to consider how you can utilize these photographs in your marketing and save them in a format that makes them easily accessible.

Ensuring You Have the Appropriate Photos.

If you have other images to use, make it clear to your photographer or layout and design person that you want them in jpeg format so they can be used online and in other formats.

Some book designers may prefer tiff photographs, which are sometimes superior for print quality, while jpeg images are usually just as good. Because the Internet likes jpegs, you won't be able to upload your tiff photographs online. Changing picture formats may not be an issue if you are familiar with Photoshop or another application that allows you to crop and modify photographs.

Alternatively, you may like to learn how to edit images to have more alternatives in the future. If you want ready-to-use photographs, be sure to inform your book layout expert that you want any cropping or alterations he makes to be duplicated exactly as they appear in your book. Hence, you have the greatest images to use in your marketing efforts. Even if your book is only printed in black and white, you must request these photographs as jpegs and in color.

In a book, black-and-white images are acceptable, but online, color is expected. In addition, photos for books are typically required to have a high quality, such as 300 dpi, whereas images posted online should have a reduced resolution, such as 72 dpi, because they will take little time to load on a web page.

Multiple Marketing Methods for Your Book Images.

If you are a first-time author launching your first website, you will want it to mirror your book's cover or reflect the substance of your book. Use themes, colors, pictures, and images that correspond with your book's tone, purpose, and content.

Use these photographs as a preview to encourage readers to purchase the book. You don't want to settle for a website that conflicts with your book cover or its graphics or utilize pre-made designs that don't present the proper image or, worse, one that is contradictory. Consult with your website's designer to make the most use of the cover and other photos.

Similar to your website, your blog should represent the concept and content of your book and your author's identity. A few photographs from your book, such as an author photo or a page, may be posted to the blog using the site's template. Then, add your remaining photographs to your blog, one or two at a time.

Here is an area where you will want to have a large number of jpeg photographs available so that if you are going to write a blog daily or even just a couple of times per week, your images are all readily available and already cropped and sized to save you time.

Post extracts from your book and accompanies them with appropriate book photos. Alternate postings from your book with posts about yourself or things you've done, and continue to snap and publish your images.

Effective blogging with images may necessitate you to learn how to use a program such as Fireworks or Photoshop so that your photographs are of excellent quality and cropped or edited for optimal effect.

Because viewers will likely have to scroll down to read the entirety of your blog post, include an image at the top of the post so that it immediately attracts attention rather than burying it further down the page and teasing your viewers by posting one or two of your greatest photographs from a chapter and letting them know that there are more images in the book.

In the age of social networking, people like perusing each other's online photo albums. Whether on Facebook, Instagram, TikTok, or another site that allows you to add photos or images to an album, establish a photo album for your book, or multiple albums for different portions of your book. People will be more interested in your book if there are photographs included. Also, feel free to use some of these photographs as your profile.

Book Preview Videos: Create a book preview video. Reader Views is a professional book promotion firm that produces book preview films for authors. You will need to submit a dozen or more of your book's finest photographs in jpeg format to be utilized in the movie.

You may want to include a voiceover script or have one created to help you match the spoken words with the appropriate photos. Even if your book does not contain many photographs, here is a reason to discover more images that will help you promote the book, provided you pay for them or use royalty-free images.

Postcards and Other Marketing Materials: Consider all book promotion options beyond the ones listed above. If you've authored a history or travel book, you may like to transform your photographs into a line of postcards.

If tourists are inclined to purchase your book, they will also purchase your postcards. Because postcards are typically inexpensive, you may be able to sell a significant number of them. Choose five or six of your best photographs and create a bookmarker series; for children's novels, you may create a bookmarker for each of the book's characters.

What about note cards, posters, calendars, children's trading cards, coffee mugs, tote bags, jigsaw puzzles, and perhaps a line of T-shirts? Even if you do not mention your book on all these things, you may generate additional cash from your photographs and sell these products in addition to your book on your website.

The neighborhood gift shop may not be interested in selling your books, but they may be interested in selling your calendars or t-shirts. Do not restrict yourself. Promote and sell your photographs, with or without the book.

Images are essential to the marketing of a book. People enjoy looking at photos, and they will capture the reader's attention when simple text may not. Utilize your photographs to attract interest and market your book in every manner possible. Be imaginative so that these photographs can generate more cash as an author.

CHAPTER 6: HOW TO PROMOTE YOUR CHILDREN'S EBOOK THROUGH SPEAKING ENGAGEMENTS.

Traditionally, authors releasing a new book would embark on a "book tour" consisting of signings, presentations, speeches, and media interviews across the nation. Although many of these activities have shifted online during the past decade, speaking engagements are an effective method for selling books and building an audience.

There is no reason why Kindle writers cannot enjoy these advantages, even if they do not have physical copies to sell in the back of the room or to hold up at the podium.

Localize your Kindle speaking tour. Each municipality or group has a chamber of commerce and continually seeks breakfast or luncheon speakers. In many regions, there are also independent local networking organizations.

If you are unfamiliar with the networking environment in your community, speak with a local banker, real estate agent, or owner of a local service business or inquire at the closest Small Business Development Center or community development office.

Your book's subject matter may appeal to specialist groups, such as garden clubs, political organizations, and churches. Examine the event calendars in your local newspaper or online to learn which organizations routinely host public events with speakers.

Create a list of organizations that may be eager to have you speak for them. For each, call or email the organization and inquire about the speaking coordinator's name and contact information.

Then contact that person by phone or email and offer your services as a speaker. Include a brief bio, a description of your Kindle ebook, and a summary of the topic you intend to discuss and why it would interest the group's members. Typically, the following step is to establish a date for your discussion.

In addition, most public libraries feature a meeting room where they permit or welcome speaking engagements. Visit the library in your community and inquire as to who organizes meetings. Make an introduction and offer to speak. This has always worked for me wherever I've lived.

You can also contact local businesses with conference rooms if they would like to host a small speaking event for their clients. Describe how this promotes them as helpful in their clients' perspective. Your topic should not directly relate to the work of these professionals for this strategy to be effective.

For example, if your booklet teaches parents how to assist their children in developing better study skills, a lawyer, accountant, or therapist would be serving their clients who have children by hosting your speak on this topic at their office.

Non-local activities take far more planning, as they must be scheduled around your availability to travel to a certain location.

Some ebook authors struggle because they have nothing tangible to sell during their speaking engagements. How do you then urge attendees to purchase? Simple! Create flyers with what is known as a QR code (if you Google "free QR code generator," you can find websites where you can generate one for your ebook).

Those in the audience who possess smartphones can scan the QR code to access the ebook's sales page. Include a conventional URL for your sales page on the flyer for individuals without smartphones. They will bring the flyer home and purchase your ebook on their home computer.

Send a press release to local newspapers whenever you perform the above actions if the event is accessible to the public. Often, a speaking engagement is an excuse for a lengthy article on the book or business in question. This can generate sales from individuals who did not attend your presentation.

CHAPTER 7: HOW TO CONSTRUCT YOUR AUTHOR PLATFORM TO IMPROVE CHILDREN'S BOOK PROMOTION.

As a children's book author, you've likely encountered the term author platform often, but you may be wondering: what is a platform, and how can I get one?

Your author platform determines your market reach and is vital for your book marketing efforts. If you wish to secure a book deal with a typical commercial publisher, you must have a solid author platform. When evaluating book proposals, publishers want to know how well-known you are and how effective you will be at advertising your book after publication.

Before you write a book or book proposal is the ideal moment to begin constructing your author platform, as it needs time. However, you may continue to build your author platform regardless of where you are in the publishing process.

There are many definitions of author platform, but they all boil down to three elements:

- Branding.

- Reputation.

- Networking.

Branding.

Branding distinguishes you in a crowded market and makes you memorable. Your author tagline is one of the most significant aspects of your brand; it is a concise and engaging representation of what you do.

The following are examples of author taglines:

- The Publicity Hound.
- The Love Doctor.
- The Productivity Pro.
- The Risqué Romance Author.
- Author of suspenseful mysteries.
- Author of the Detective McGee series.
- Author of instructive books for children.

Use your slogan as a title, following your name in advertising materials and your signature. I refer to myself, for instance, as Dana Lynn Smith, The Savvy Book Marketer.

Your author photo is an additional promotional asset. Get a professional-looking photograph and utilize it everywhere to increase your visibility.

Professional does not necessarily imply a studio image; consider how your author photo's background, pose, and attire might reflect your brand and the genres of books you write. Wherever your photo appears, always provide a caption with your name and tagline.

Author branding can include your logo, book covers, color scheme, particular writing or speaking style, and academic credentials. Together, these features generate a recognizable brand that makes you memorable and improves the credibility of your author platform.

Consider the steps you may take to improve your brand.

Reputation.

Reputation is a measurement of how well-known you are, what you're known for, and your credibility. Consider the following considerations when promoting your book:

- Do you have a degree, training, or substantial experience in the subject you're writing about and/or writing?
- Do you hold a professional qualification in your area of expertise, or can you earn one?
- What honors or distinctions have you received?
- What media experience do you possess?
- How many people do your monthly speeches and interviews reach?
- How many individuals visit your blog?
- How many articles have you authored, posted, or published in the past month?
- How well-known are you, and how recognizable is your name?
- What roles of leadership do you hold?
- Why should individuals listen to you or read your works?

Nonfiction authors can develop a reputation as an authority on their subject through activities such as producing books and articles, giving speeches and teaching, appearing on talk programs, being mentioned in other authors' publications, and penning the forewords of other books.

Fiction authors may become well-known for their writing style and proficiency in a particular genre (such as children's, science fiction, romance, or mystery) or specialization within a genre (vampire stories, romantic adventure).

Your author platform and reputation can be bolstered by winning accolades, gaining outstanding book reviews, and receiving testimonials and endorsements from celebrities and industry professionals.

What can you do to improve the number of people you reach with your book promotion efforts and boost your author reputation and expert status?

How can your marketing materials highlight your credentials?

Connections.

When promoting a book, who you know is more important than what you know!

To sell books in the current market, you must be linked. Here are a few examples of connections that authors might utilize to promote their books:

- Contact Database - Clients, leads, coworkers, friends, and family.

- Opt-in Mailing List – Individuals who have authorized you to contact them.

- Influencers - Celebrities, notable individuals in your industry, book reviews, the media, and bloggers.

- Connections on Facebook, Twitter, and other online social networks, groups, and forums.

- Blog Readers - Individuals who view your blog or subscribe to its feed.

- Professional Associations - Members and leaders of the association. Leadership positions increase one's visibility inside a company.

- Other Organizations - Alumni associations, civic and service groups, hobbies clubs, etc.

CHAPTER 8: WHY SOME AUTHORS NEVER SUCCEED AS CHILDREN'S AUTHORS.

1 - Being Overly interested in the Outcome - Nobody wants to believe that the book they've labored on for hours, weeks, or months will fail. It is inevitable, and you must be ready for it.

The books you consider your finest work will fail to gain traction, while those you created with half the effort will soar higher than you ever imagined. This could result from riding the newest trend, a stroke of luck, or other unknown circumstances.

Not to be taken personally. Many budding authors give up when their first book fails to meet their expectations. Even if you've done everything in your power to help your latest product succeed, it might be difficult to observe its failure.

If you've exhausted all possible options, draw a line in the sand and move on to the next endeavor. Too many authors waste money trying to make something that will never be successful. Don't become overly attached to the outcome.

2 - Anticipating Retirement After Publishing One Book - In contrast to Hollywood films in which the protagonist types "The End" on the final page of their manuscript and it sells like hotcakes, life sadly follows its own rules, and one of them is that you must exert effort to get good fortune. Compared to the hundreds or thousands of books published each week, your book is a drop in the ocean: generosity.

If you compare a website with one page to one with ten, twenty, or one hundred pages, it is obvious that the website with the bigger number of pages will be discovered by more people but do not be discouraged. You can increase your book's chances of success by distributing it to as many online and retail bookstores as possible. The more locations where people can find you, the better.

So, discard the notion that a single book will suffice. Work on your second and third drafts. Then, when you do connect with your audience, you will have even more books for them to devour.

3 - Never Asking For Reviews - Let's face it, not all of us are the sales type, so the idea of venturing beyond our circle of friends and family to peddle our latest masterpiece might be daunting, but if you're plagued by thoughts such as "What if people don't like it?" and "What if the only reviews I get are negative?" you'll never be able to release your work. You're doomed to failure.

If you wish to be successful in the publishing industry, you must be prepared for the possibility that not everyone will like your book or even you. These individuals have raised their hands and stated, "I am not your audience." Then, your goal is to find your audience. You are doing yourself a great disservice by not requesting reviews or putting your book in front of many people as possible.

4 - Going It Alone - Have you ever observed a performer spinning plates? You observe with astonishment as they run from one slowing plate to another, speeding it up and balancing it before running back to the first. If this describes you and your writing, it is only time before everything collapses and you give up in despair.

Every large publishing house has teams that do the many tasks necessary to generate and market a book. Before a book reaches the shelves, it is reviewed by proofreaders, editors, designers, illustrators, and a marketing group. If you wear all those hats, your novels will never be as successful as they could be. I know from personal experience.

If you don't have the resources to hire someone for all these activities, start small and identify somebody who can handle your weakest responsibilities. Go to Fiverr.com and hire someone to create your book covers if you do not want to create your own.

Then, hire someone with copywriting skills to compose your book's blurbs and descriptions, followed by a specialist in book promotion. It need not be complex or expensive. The longer you continue to play all these roles, the longer it will take you to achieve success.

Not examine your writing as a business owner would - McDonald's would never open a restaurant in an area where no one walked, Walmart would never load its shelves with things that nobody desired, and Amazon would never sell you a single item on your way to the checkout page.

However, how many authors commit these errors? Writing for an audience that does not exist, publishing books that nobody wants, and having only one book to sell as opposed to a series. Too many, and this is how you should focus on your writing and books going forward.

If something is ineffective, causing you to lose money or consuming too much of your time, let it go and move on. Concentrate your time and energy on what is working and repeat the procedure.

If a book is successful, create a sequel, prequel, or any other sequel that will provide additional revenue. If you spent $100 to promote your last book and only made $50, I'm sure I don't have to tell you that was a poor business decision.

In the end, a book is an asset, nothing more and nothing less. Reject the notion that it is a piece of art or an indication of who you are. People who have such views live the life of a hungry artist—people who view their books as a company that is either profitable or unprofitable don't.

CHAPTER 9: SUBMISSIONS TO CONTRACT TO BOOK MARKETING TO WRITING PROFESSION.

Learning the craft of writing is the cornerstone of writing novels for children or any genre. As a children's author, you must grasp the unique guidelines and techniques for writing age-appropriate stories with age-appropriate vocabulary and plots.

Once you have taken the time to master your skill and have evaluated, revised, and edited your manuscript, the traditional writing books for children writing road continue with submissions, promotion, and a writing career.

Writing Children's Books: Submissions.

Before you consider submitting your work anywhere, ensure that you have taken the essential measures to master the craft of writing. Your manuscript should be as well polished as possible.

There are two types of submissions: those to publishers and those to agencies. In I recommended "researching agents" before submitting to them.

Before submitting a question to an agent, you should know your intentions, especially before appending a contract signature. This involves determining the agent type they are the genre they represent, and the agent platform they offer: do they satisfy their authors or crack the whip? Are they passive, aggressive, involved, or complacent?

The same advice applies to submitting to publishers; before submitting to publishers, conduct research on them. Know which genres of children's books they publish and the types of plots they seek.

Whether sending to a publisher or an agent, you must always adhere to the submission requirements and personalize the question. There may be instances where the guidelines do not specify the editor's name to whom the question should be sent, but if you can find this information, utilize it.

Knowing how to pitch your tale is equally essential. This involves discovering the story's hook. Agents and publishers are also interested in the book's selling elements and similarities to other successful publications.

In addition, they will anticipate being informed of your marketing approach. Before submitting your work, you should establish an internet presence and platform; inform agents and publishers that you will aggressively promote your book.

In addition to the tale's hook, you must convey: who your main character is and what he or she is about; the action that propels the story; the main character's difficulty; and, if the obstacle is not overcome, what's at stake.

Examine "the back of published books" to determine how concisely and effectively they express the story's substance. This provides you with an example of how to write your summary.

Keep your question brief and professional, and keep your bio concise and pertinent. You must captivate the editor or agent and entice them to read your manuscript.

Here are four tools that can assist you in your search for a publisher or agent:

1. Where to Sell Your Work and How to Do It.

Over 700 listings for book publishers, journals, agents, art representatives, and more. WritersMarket.com is an online platform that can help you market your writing.

2. The Book Contract.

If you do your research, your novel will find a home eventually. If you receive your first rejections, don't let them discourage you. A published author may not even be the best writer, but she is undoubtedly a persistent author.

You should request an explanation if you don't understand something in your contract. After signing a contract, you will be "placed in line" and will begin editing with the publisher's editor at some point. One to two years can pass between the beginning of the publication procedure and its actual release.

3. Book Promotion.

A few months before the release of your book, you should begin promoting it to boost sales. This will need creating an author website and platform; you will need to promote yourself and your work.

After the publication of your book, you will need to engage in virtual book tours, blog talk radio guest spots, school visits, and other typical book promotion techniques. You may either handle this on your own or engage a book promotion business or publicist.

4. A Writing Career.

Now that you have your book, you are pushing it like crazy (this is an ongoing process). The final and subsequent stage is to repeat the procedure. You won't want to be a one-hit wonder, so I hope you've been penning further pieces. If not, start immediately. An author publishes a book every one to two years on average.

In addition to maintaining your enthusiasm for creating children's books, publishing books opens the door to other writing options, such as speaking engagements, workshops and/or teleseminars, and coaching.

Many marketers assert that your 'book' is your business card or calling card; it demonstrates your capabilities and promotes you as an authority in your profession or specialty. Take advantage of these new channels of exposure and revenue.

CHAPTER 10: ONLINE BOOK MARKETING.

If you have completed the book launch, press releases, media interviews, library talks, store signings, school visits, etc., and are unsure of what to do next, you may wish to promote your book online.

Millions of websites and blogs are geared toward book readers, authors, educators, children, adolescents, etc., and hundreds (if not thousands) more address each of the topics and concerns discussed in your book.

Consider each website and blog as a "virtual venue" for promoting your book.

There are two primary techniques to accomplish this:

1. The website or blog owner (or a staff member) will email you a series of questions, and you

will respond via email. Then, your (potentially modified) responses to their questions are placed on their website. They may also promote it in their newsletter or e-zine or urge their subscribers to submit questions for you.

2. Pieces: You arrange to write one or more brief articles for publication on their website or newsletter.

After each interview or article, you may mention your book and where it may be purchased. That is your compensation. You should not expect compensation for the interview or piece itself; you're doing it for publicity, not money.

Create a list of everything your book covers, including the primary theme, subtopics, locales, issues, etc. Include the things you investigated while writing the book, even if they were cut from the final draft.

There will be more areas about which you now have some insider knowledge, such as book authoring, finding an agent or publisher, possibly self-publishing, locating and collaborating with a cover artist, delivering speeches, book signings, etc. You may likely be astonished by the size of your final list.

Each of these themes will be covered by an astounding number of websites and blogs, and many of these internet platforms will seek fresh content. Therefore, utilize your preferred search engine to research each item on your list.

There will likely be millions of results for each topic. Consider the first two pages of the search results and select a handful of the most relevant websites. Then, send an email to the site owners asking if they would want to conduct an interview with you or have you write a relevant piece for their site.

Document the sites you've contacted and their responses (if any). If any larger sites do not answer, try again a week later and possibly a week after. You could also explore contacting them via phone or snail mail instead of email.

Don't give up on those large websites until you receive a definitive "Yes" or "No" - they likely receive thousands of visitors. Imagine a book signing in the real world attended by thousands of people. You don't want such a chance lost because the site owner was too busy to respond to your email.

Online book promotion has some significant advantages over attending promotional events in person.

- No travel is involved, saving you substantial time and money.

- You will never run out of venues; simply on to the next page of search results or the next item on your list.

- Multiple places can be visited in one day.

- You may cover a far larger area - the entire planet.

- Even the smallest online venue typically has a significantly greater audience than a single book signing event in person.

- Your post or interview will typically remain online and continue to generate revenue for years.

- You do not need to have a wonderful speaking voice or the ability to think of quick responses.

Once you've completed a few of these articles or interviews, it will become much simpler, as you can recycle the same fundamental comments and concepts with little modifications.

However, as no two presentations or interviews in the real world are identical, you should strive to make each online event unique. Try to adapt your writing to each website's tone and audience.

Consider how much time you would spend preparing for, traveling to, and presenting at a similar event in the real world. You'll be able to complete the online event in a fraction of the time and likely get much better outcomes - all without leaving your desk.

CHAPTER 11; ENSURE YOU HAVE A REMARKABLE BOOK COVER.

It is said that you can judge a book by its cover. Not exactly right. There might be excellent books with poor and average books with excellent covers. There is one certainty. Excellent book covers sell books.

I've had a few books where one cover worked exceptionally well, and the other did not. My mistake was attempting to brand a series by the same author by attempting to match the design of the second book to that of the first.

The trouble was that the second book was about a different subject and required a different approach. The following time, I will rely on professional experience and provide input regarding the target market. I do have some comments regarding the style of the cover, however.

I adore simplicity and daring. I want the purchaser to recognize the title and topic of the book immediately. I want the title and sub-title to be clear unless the sub-title is intended to elucidate the content. I speak from personal experience.

I published a book on essay writing titled I Wish I'd Had This When I Was in School well over a decade ago. Even though the title was large and bold, it did not indicate the book's substance. The title of your book must convey a distinct personality, especially in the non-fiction sector.

Overstuffing a cover with too much content is the one thing I have avoided. We've all seen book covers where every square inch is loaded with either graphics or promotional text. It's excessive. Also, it cannot be read from a distance. I would like a buyer to be able to read that title from at least three to four yards away at a bookstore.

This leads me to my next point: white space. Pages with excessive text want white space. Now, I'm not recommending that you use white as a background for a book cover, although, as you might guess, it works exceptionally well for some books.

Some authors advise using "a color, a texture or a backdrop illustration instead." In addition, white space is required, but not a white background.

What I did not do when selecting a design for a business book was take a close look at similar book covers. I did check out price comparisons but not cover designs. Visit your local bookshop if you're currently reading a business book, a children's book, or any other genre. It exists a pattern that strikes your eye that could function, if only as a broad concept, for your forthcoming book?

One last piece of advice is to speak with a local publisher. A few years ago, I attended a conference at which a prominent publisher gave a presentation on the design and requested attendees to submit their books for evaluation.

I wish that dialogue had occurred before publishing one of my novels. The content was excellent. However, a better cover would have increased sales. This is a lesson I would like to impart to you.

Excellent book covers sell books.

CHAPTER 12: SUGGESTIONS FOR FINDING CHILDREN'S BOOK PUBLISHERS.

The number of individuals who believe they will create a children's book because it is simple will tell you that writing is difficult. When you have a written story that you believe would be a success in the children's market, you will need to find a publisher specializing in that kind of writing; you need a children's book publisher.

To ensure that you discover a publisher who shares your enthusiasm for entertaining and teaching children, there are some aspects you must consider when selecting children's book publishers.

Putting together a superb paper should be your priority. The desire for self-publishing has increased dramatically over the past years since publishers no longer accept many new authors but instead work with established authors. Getting a foot in the door with any children's book publisher begins with submitting an outstanding manuscript. You want them to read your article, determine its value and offer to publish it on your behalf.

Find publishing houses that specialize in children's literature. Not all publishers have expertise in publishing children's books. Because this is such a niche market, you must find a publisher who will focus on getting your book into retailers for the appropriate age group.

When selecting a publisher for a children's book, it is essential to find a publishing business with a solid reputation in the children's market. You must ensure that the publisher you select will help you advertise your book and ensure that it reaches the appropriate audience in the future. Do not accept a contract from any publisher; instead, wait to see what everyone offers so you may choose the best option.

Throughout this procedure, you must remember that publishers are no longer accepting all books. In reality, going through a publishing house can be extremely intimidating because you need an agent to approach the publishing houses on your behalf, which can be lengthy and laborious. This is why self-publishing has become such a popular business, allowing authors to publish and distribute their work on schedule.

Self-publishing allows you to maintain complete control over your work. You choose the method of publication, whether a book is printed or published online. You can make judgments based on what you believe to be optimal for your job and the optimal method for distributing it.

Self-publishing allows you to efficiently control your future with the assistance of an experienced publisher who can provide you with a plethora of guidance and assistance.

Utilize the author assistance tools with which self-publishing pros can assist you. When publishing a children's book, you'll need a captivating front cover and pictures to keep the child's attention.

The publishing company you select should be able to provide you with helpful guidance, have in-house designers to assist with illustrations and front cover design, and provide proofreading and editing as an extra convenience.

Always remember, while searching for children's book publishers, to take the time to learn as much as possible about the company through internet reviews and client feedback, so you can confidently decide what to do with your work.

CHAPTER 13: WRITING FOR CHILDREN AND WINNING OVER PARENTS.

The talent of being able to communicate in a language that your target audience speaks is an obvious one. Choosing a subject that the child can relate to is crucial. Again, depending on the child's age, it is often believed necessary to include visuals; yet, children of all ages like seeing illustrations.

You must comprehend what the children and their parents desire from reading. It is crucial to maintain the children's happiness and enjoyment of the story while appealing to their creativity and creative energy but what will convince the parents to purchase the book?

Parents are also looking for books with educational value for their children. New words and concepts are instructive in and of themselves. Still, parents often want something more tangible - a means to quantify the book's success in terms of its educational worth for their children.

Including activities within the book's text might give it a distinctive quality that will appeal to both children and their parents. A glossary of unfamiliar or uncommon words can guarantee that children and parents properly comprehend the material and that youngsters are not constantly wondering what a particular word means.

A huge book containing stories and activities was a common Christmas present in the past. These Annuals were always popular since they included different activities for children to complete while reading the stories. Adding quizzes, crossword puzzles, writing, and drawing/coloring exercises improve the story for children and their parents.

Currently, books with more activities than narratives are gaining market share. Still, if you combine your talent for storytelling with appropriate, entertaining activities, you will appeal to both children and their parents and increase the likelihood of success for your writing.

With the Internet, producing e-books with full-color graphics is possible without being constrained by production expenses. This, of course, implies that your books may be less expensive than those sold in stores.

This is a more complex process regarding advertising and marketing your book to generate sales. Internet marketers generally agree, however, that writing and publishing articles are one of the finest methods to establish credibility as a children's author. Include a reference box at the end of the piece with a link to your website (or email) where the book can be purchased.

You have an advantage over others because you can write and produce an article that would be "no big trouble." Ensure that you send your post to the appropriate e-zine, newsletter, or category on web sites such as this one - you need to target customers who have children, for instance. Mums.

If you decide to approach your church or school, try establishing an affiliate program in which the organization receives a commission (about 50 percent) for promoting your book for you, such as through a testimonial.

Don't worry about offering big commissions; you have no additional expenses after you've written your book. This is a wonderful method to demonstrate your community spirit and improve your reputation as a compassionate children's author. The parents will value your kindness, while the youngsters will enjoy your book.

CHAPTER 14; BOOSTING THE VISIBILITY OF YOUR SELF-PUBLISHED CHILDREN'S BOOK.

Congratulations! You just released your children's book independently! Now, how do you get it out to the public? Promoting your book needs much work and persistence. Success will not occur overnight, regardless of how much you want for it. Below are some approaches I have implemented or planned to promote my children's books.

1. Establish a website. Display your book! Create a PDF file of your book's preview! Most buyers will want a preview before purchasing, so provide one. Create a link via which people can purchase your book.

2. Create a blog and network with other authors.

3. Create a fan page on Facebook and a Twitter account. Introduce your Facebook fan page to your pals. Follow individuals on Twitter who share your interests. Facebook advertising is also possible, but only if you have sufficient finances.

4. Get reviews. Request that other self-published authors of children's books review your book in exchange for reviewing theirs. Post these testimonials on your blog or website.

5. Visiting cards! Go to Vistaprint.com. You can submit your templates or utilize theirs. Distribute business cards whenever possible. If you have children, bring them to the park and distribute them to other parents.

6. If your children's book is part of a series, offer the first installment on eBay. I had the most views and bids when I began with a starting price of $0.01 and free shipping. You will likely incur a financial loss, but your book will be acquired by a reader who has never read it. Offer a discount on your

other books if customers enjoy the first one. Include your business card as well!

7. Write letters to daycares and libraries outlining your book and why they should have it. If possible, offer them a special discount.

8. Stickers or magnets for your car's bumper! Design it as you see fit, and be sure to include your website!

9. Attach flyers with tear-off tabs to bulletin boards. Many grocery stores and libraries have them. Try the pizza joints as well! You may need to inquire before hanging up. Ensure that you check on them at least weekly. (*Tear a tab off. This will provide the impression that folks are interested in your flyer. This has been tried, and it works!*)

Some websites offer inexpensive advertising! They provide a banner swap service, but you can also purchase banner impressions and website clicks. Websites add a code to their site, and when someone visits their site, they receive a banner view on another website.

Therefore, when you purchase clicks, you are paying for people to click on your banners. Therefore, these are actual people who clicked on your banner because it caught their attention. Examine the effectiveness of a low-cost campaign by implementing it.

CHAPTER 15: MAKING YOUR CHILDREN'S BOOK A BESTSELLER.

Congratulations! You have published a book for youngsters. Now, the next and most crucial phase is Promotion. Children are devoted readers but first tough to engage. This page lists websites that promote children's and young adult literature.

1. Bookmarket - This is a page that provides promotion-related advice. The book 1001 ways to advertise your book by John Kremer is a valuable resource for all authors. Children's writer's and illustrator's market by Writer's Digest includes a list of publishers and writing tips.

2. Reviews are an excellent method to advertise your book. It assists your book considerably. Send requests for giveaways, reviews, and interviews to all blogs and websites, no matter their size.

3. Read your book in a local children's library or contribute a copy to a school. You can leave books wherever youngsters frequent.

4. A podcast and trailer effectively market a book. The remedy for children who are too lazy to read is a podcast.

5. Script - Scriptwriting is considered entirely distinct from novel writing. Most popular books are adapted into films and radio broadcasts. Nevertheless, you can utilize this strategy to advertise your book.

6. The BBC and other broadcasters accept submissions. However, acceptance is often challenging. Many scriptwriting competitions are also open to amateur authors. Children enjoy television viewing.

7. Testimonials Famous people's endorsements can benefit your book.

8. This is a terrific method to let children know your book has been published. This is more effective for literature intended for an older audience. Announce the publication of your book in a children's magazine or newspaper. This may incur costs. In addition, you may write for a children's magazine or conduct interviews to promote your book.

9. Flyers, posters, etc. - These need money to print but can be successful, particularly with children.

10. Advertising on websites that feature your book's content or content similar to your book's content will increase sales. Advertising on television is the most effective technique to attract children's attention, but it is expensive, and children may not enjoy seeing book advertisements.

11. Be featured in catalogs of children's books.

Website prizes and literary accolades can assist increase book sales. Again, this is problematic since literary awards have stringent selection standards.

Many librarians like to purchase award-winning publications. This also increases the book's visibility.

Many youngsters develop the habit of reading books from their library collection. For children under the age of twelve, the school library is the gateway to the world of literature.

Ensure that your books are available in public and even school libraries. Children have limited purchasing power, but if they enjoy one of your free books and decide to purchase others, there is a chance they will do so.

Typically, I would advocate social networking, but if your works are intended for children under twelve, it is pointless. Promote on the websites of both teachers and students. Recommend it for class reading assignments or book weeks. Try to exert much influence on the people and schools in your vicinity.

As most children's internet watching is filtered, websites are not very useful for children. Therefore, I also do not recommend electronic literature to kids.

Teenagers are more receptive to e-books and influenced by the internet. Also, although money is essential, it does not significantly influence children's novels relative to adult publications.

CHAPTER 16: UTILIZING CUSTOM-MADE BOBBLE HEADS FOR PROMOTION.

Some individuals sell a product. Others constitute the product. To get fresh possibilities, you must engage in self-promotion if you are a writer, singer, politician, artist, in the public eye, or otherwise self-employed. You have an identity card. You have dispersed flyers. You need a novel way to reach out to prospective clients and constituents.

Consider custom figures!

Why Order Custom Bobble Heads?

These figurines not only put your name in front of the public but also put you in front of the public. A handcrafted figurine delivers greater name recognition than a pencil or matchbook for a politician who wants to maintain accessibility. If you're a writer, artist, or musician competing with other aspiring writers, painters, and musicians for attention, a figurine stands head and shoulders over posters and bookmarks.

Personal figurines build a connection between you and your audience. Because the face of the figure is typically a caricature, it also provides humor, making you more approachable. You are not Senator Smith; you are my pleasant and nice Senator Smith. You are not the guitarist Crash Jones; you are a fun-loving member of a fantastic band.

A personalized bobblehead is also uncommon. You will be remembered when you include one in your press kit or distribute it at events. Because figurines are durable, prospective customers will remember you long after the competition's business cards and calendars have been discarded.

How to Advertise Using a Bobble-Head.

A customized bobblehead is an adaptable instrument. Add this to your press kit. Distribute it at concerts, exhibits, rallies, conventions, book signings, festivals, and fairs. Use it as a reward for blog contests and a giveaway for online and actual tours. Include it in promotional gift baskets, goodie bags, and appreciation gifts.

A personalized figurine of your main character can attract children to your table during a book signing if you have authored a novel. Regardless of your business, never hesitate to utilize your doll as a present for youngsters.

You will be remembered as unkind if you refuse. On the other side, if you give a bobblehead to a youngster who requests one, you will be perceived as a generous child-lover, which is always a positive image.

Whenever you make a personal appearance, whether at a school, campaign stop, reading, or sales call, have your figurine and information package readily available. You never know when a promotional opportunity will present itself.

Selecting Your Custom Figurine:

- What should the look of your bobblehead be?

- Is it a carbon copy of yourself, your group, or your personality?

- What actions should your figure perform?

- Do you need a backdrop?

- How much information do you need?

Find a production company that recognizes and promotes your vision when selecting one.

Choose a company that needs your consent on each production step. Ensure that your personalized bobblehead will be made with safe, long-lasting materials. Consider a company's experience, reputation for quality, and customer service.

When you are the product, you need the most effective advertising. Include a customized bobblehead in your promotional materials!

CHAPTER 17: CONSIDERATIONS TO MAKE BEFORE PUBLISHING A CHILDREN'S EBOOK.

I believed that writing a children's book would be simple. I employed my mature mind. After searching the Internet for suggestions on how to write children's books, I discovered that simply sitting at my computer was insufficient.

First, I had to establish the age group I wished to appeal to. Children's vocabulary and interest span vary between the ages of five and eight, nine and twelve, and thirteen and fifteen.

I spent a day in the children's area of the bookshop examining the language each age group could comprehend, the type and quantity of illustrations, the length of the books, the topics of interest for each age group, and how the children in the section interacted with their selections.

Next, I had to decide what genre I wanted to write in (adventure, fantasy, science fiction, personal experience, etc.) and the book-length criteria. Online descriptions exist for each of these factors. I searched websites for fantasy and science fiction books to see what subjects other authors have written on. Which novels were awarded prizes and why?

I also researched the trends in graphic and image styles used for each age group on websites for children's books. Since I was preparing to become a teacher, I also used teachers' resources to see which textbooks were used for kids of various ages.

The Amazon, Barnes & Noble, and Borders websites were also useful tools for demonstrating which books were the most popular among the various age groups. The printed approach was too time-consuming, expensive, and intimidating at this stage, so I chose to self-publish online. In the Kindle

Book Publishing section of Amazon's website, budding Kindle authors will find enough support.

For marketing my eBook, I invested in online services that instruct you on using blogs, advertising, and publishing tactics to attract buyers to your book. In addition, you will learn how to price your Ebook, how many people have accessed your book's description, and how to track the promotional rankings. You can also create a website to encourage people to buy your book.

Depending on where you intend to sell your book, you must format it according to the guidelines. Follow these guidelines carefully if you wish for your book to be effortlessly readable. I've seen books with strange symbols interspersed throughout the text. Some services will do everything for a fee and the option to do it yourself. Using a website, I developed a cover for use with my Amazon description.

This is merely an introduction to writing, publishing, and selling children's eBooks. I am confident that you may find many more online resources that provide your needed information. Allow your imagination to flow freely but always keep your intended audience in mind as you write.

CHAPTER 18; BOOK MARKETING TIPS THAT WILL HELP YOU SELL MORE COPIES.

There has never been a best-selling book without some form of effort. Even legendary authors were put through the wringer before publication and widespread readership. It needs effort, perseverance, and book marketing strategies to go from unknown writer to best-selling author. Here are five of these marketing ideas for consideration.

1. Increase your internet visibility. If you do not have a website, create one. Join a social media community if you're not already involved in one. Include a testimonial page on your website, get individuals to review your book on your Facebook page, become visible on Twitter, consider hosting Q&A sessions on Google+, and optimize your website for search engines.

People learn more about new books from the Internet, friends, bookstores, or advertisements. Social networking platforms have increased the quantity of word-of-mouth advertising, allowing readers to discover new authors. Therefore, expand your internet presence.

2. Do not let technology and trends deter you from implementing ebook marketing. Many authors now offer ebook editions of their works. Adult fiction has propelled ebook revenues to $1.27 billion in a couple of years, according to BookStats, while children's ebook sales have tripled in the same time frame. With 84 million iPads sold globally and reading tablets increasing their product deliveries, you should not overlook the lucrative potential of electronic book marketing.

3. Entrust an expert with your ebook strategy. You can receive many submissions of your book to top-tier ebook marketing websites, Twitter campaigns, and other strategic efforts, such as a

competition for a fan review, for the cheapest expenditure possible to increase your book's exposure.

4. Explore your book on the web. Promote your book on blog sites associated with your genre or specific market. This is a wonderful method for attracting people to your book and helping them to spread the word about it across their networks. When you expand a community, you eventually amass a following.

5. Develop your internet reputation and become an authority. This is particularly crucial for authors of self-help and how-to books. Develop web videos. Learn about how to become active on LinkedIn Answers.

6. Never pass up an opportunity to answer questions from fans regarding your book. When you gain sufficient recognition for your credentials and expertise on a particular subject, your book (or books) will be pushed without difficulty.

Marketing an ebook or a book for the online market might have lucrative results. You must simply exert effort. Be Web savvy. Rely on a specialist for assistance with your campaigns. Develop your brand, and who knows, perhaps the book you completed many years ago will help you become a best-selling author today.

CHAPTER 19: BOOK PROMOTION MISTAKES TO AVOID.

There are hundreds of professionals out there writing, blogging, and speaking about what authors should do to sell their novels, but sometimes, authors also need to hear about what they should avoid doing.

I've compiled a handful of the craziest tales I've heard about authors writing or promoting their novels, and while they may seem ludicrous, I assure you they are all true. On the off chance that you could be on the path to insane authorship, here are a few tips on what not to do:

Bookstore Mistakes:

These two stories were recounted to me by a bookshop manager friend:

We decided to carry on consignment this author's book. So long as a book sells, we will continue to stock it. However, one author did not sell any books, so I informed him that we could no longer stock his book after six months.

He reported to me that he had sold twenty books in my shop. I informed him that the eight books we had originally stolen from him were still present. He said that he had been renewing the stack every couple of weeks.

We do not have a computerized inventory system, so when he refilled his stack, we had no method of keeping track of the books that had been sold. Thus, I cannot pay him for those volumes. In conclusion, before leaving new books in the store, verify with the bookstore manager.

We placed the books of a local author in the local book section. When I entered the store one day, all of her books were displayed alongside the bestsellers at the front table. They were returned to the local author section.

When the scenario arose again, I stressed to the author that buyers seeking local books would have difficulty locating her works if they were not in the local area, but this did not appear to make a difference.

When I returned to the office a few days later, her books were back on the front table. After relocating them several times, I called the author and informed her that we would no longer sell her books.

Festivals:

This tale was shared with me by a writer who attended an art fair:

I shared a table at an art fair with another author. Her story had recently been adapted into an audiobook. As a means of self-promotion, she decided to bring headphones so anyone could stop by and listen to the audiobook. She did not, however, stop there.

She stood outside the booth and hurried to passersby, placing headphones on their heads without permission and yelling, "Listen to my book!" She prevented people from approaching the booth to view my book, and when they saw what she was doing to other innocent visitors, they began to go out of their way to avoid us.

Interviews:

I can't count the number of times I've heard the following from authors during interviews. It does not make an interviewer happy:

"Why does your character Mary decide to? In your novel?"

To discover, you'll have to read the book.

"However, can you tell us why you chose to have Mary do it?"

"No, I fear I will reveal too much information. To discover, you'll have to read the book."

If an author cannot tell me about his or her book, I will not be interested in reading it.

Introductions to books:

One author wrote the following in the opening paragraph of his introduction:

It occurred to me that the scenarios in my novel and the fantasy world I've built would be first perplexing and difficult to follow for readers, so I decided to write this introduction to explain everything so they can follow the plot.

Telling a reader that your book is confusing will not help you sell more copies; if your book is confusing, you should continue revising it instead of publishing it.

Children's Books:

Despite your disbelief, some authors do not know what is proper for a children's book. I heard about an author whose animal protagonists investigated a murder. Worse, the murder victim was a woman, and her husband and her lover were the leading suspects. I hope murder and adultery are inappropriate topics for youngsters.

Websites:

I could list other mistakes that authors make on their websites, but this author has to earn the award for the weirdest tale ever. This is a slight paraphrase of a posting I saw on one author's website, but it represents what I've heard about more than one author (hence the blanks):

> If you want to buy my book, I can't mail it to you because _____ [the post office, the U.S. Government, the League of Evil, the aliens secretly running our planet, etc.] steals the books I've mailed on purpose so that people don't learn the truth about _____ [Bigfoot, King Arthur, the Bermuda Triangle, Jesus, etc.]. So I've converted it into a downloadable eBook on my website.

Possibly, as an author, your books are not selling as you'd like, and you're wondering what you're doing wrong. However, after reading these anecdotes, I'm confident you'll be able to congratulate yourself on the fact that you're doing at least a few things correctly.

CHAPTER 20: PROMOTE YOUR BOOK IN YOUR NEIGHBORHOOD.

Online marketing is a fantastic way to sell your book to a global audience, but writers often ignore local book marketing alternatives. You can stand out as a larger fish in a smaller pond in your local neighborhood and region. Here are five strategies for promoting your book locally:

1. Always bring reading and books with you. Keep a box of books, some flyers in your vehicle's trunk, and business cards in your wallet. You never know when you will encounter a prospective client or marketing contact.

2. Consider opportunities throughout your region. Are you going on a weekend trip or to see your grandmother? Perform preliminary research to find bookstores, businesses, and libraries in the area that

you may visit or organize your book tour, staying with family and friends along the route.

3. Promote yourself to retailers and libraries as a local author. Many bookstores and libraries provide a section that highlights the works of local or regional authors.

4. Consider alternative retailers that are a good fit. Consider which kinds of shops are relevant to the theme of your book and advertise it as the work of a local author.

5. Stick "local author" stickers on the books you sell in your community.

6. Speak at libraries. Contact libraries about presenting on the subject of your book. This is particularly useful for children's books and nonfiction titles with broad appeal (such as travel, business, or fitness). Many libraries will allow you to sell your books during your talk and others have funds for speaker compensation.

7. Find further speaking opportunities. Speaking is a terrific way to advertise your book; once you gain experience, you may even be paid to talk. Many organizations, including business and civic organizations, church groups, schools and universities, trade associations, and others, seek engaging presenters for their gatherings.

8. Pursue publicity through regional and local media. Send a press release announcing your new book to media outlets in your hometown and current residence. The "local girl makes good" approach is particularly effective in smaller communities.

9. Create press releases based on regional ties, such as a novel set in the area and current happenings. Don't forget to include your alumni newsletter and any civic or professional organizations to which you belong. Nonfiction authors should consider radio and television discussion shows.

10. Participate in book fairs and festivals. Typically, they work best if your book relates to the event's topic or has broad appeal.

11. Promote children's literature through schools and youth organizations. Visits to schools are a terrific method to reach children.

CONCLUSION.

Creating and promoting any book, particularly a children's book, is challenging. Even if traditional publication is difficult, self-publishing can lead to success. Before assuming that writing a children's book is the best course of action, it is necessary to study the present market.

There is an infinite selection of books for children. In contrast to conventional books for adults, dollar stores and bargain stores carry a vast assortment of children's books. Despite their desire for their children to receive an education, many parents prefer to spend a limited amount of money on books.

As previously indicated, competition for children's books is severe. Often, a well-known author or an engaging story, particularly for young readers or adults, drives the sale of a $15 children's book. Consequently, many publishers are cautious.

Because of this, many major publishing houses choose to continue working with the same authors or to use just agents. However, don't let this bring you down. Many publishers are prepared to take risks on new authors, and you may be one of them.

Many aspiring authors who want to be published prefer to write children's books because they believe they have a greater possibility of generating more money. Despite the possibility of variation, authors of lengthier novels and other books are often compensated more. So, is this a fact?

It is possible to write a children's book more quickly; therefore, you may be able to write more, but it is crucial to highlight that the same amount of time and consideration should be devoted to each book. Also, while writing for children, you may be able to produce more books, but they must be published before you can earn from them.

If you choose to publish a children's story, it is crucial not to restrict yourself. When many people think of children's literature, picture books and board books generally come to mind immediately.

In addition to publications for young people, there are books for beginning readers, such as short-chapter books. Remember this when attempting to write your first children's book, as you may like to experiment.

As previously mentioned, writing and publishing a children's book is not necessarily simpler, but that does not mean it is impossible. Instead of focusing on how simple it would be to publish a book or how much money you could anticipate making, you are encouraged to write about what you know or enjoy. When you are passionate about the words you write and the tale you construct, you have a much greater chance of achieving success.

With the advent of print-on-demand software and applications, producing and publishing a book is now easier. Writing a children's book is not as simple as you may believe, and getting one published through traditional channels is one of the most difficult tasks in the publishing industry.

Management Skills for Managers.

1. Time Management for Managers
2. Employee Coaching for Managers
3. Team Building for Managers
4. Self Confidence for Managers
5. Negotiation Skills for Managers
6. Customer Service Skills for Managers
7. Assertiveness for Managers
8. Business Etiquette for Managers
9. Listening Skills for Managers
10 Leadership Skills for Managers
11. Communication Skills for Managers
12. Presentation Skills for Managers
13. Stress Management for Managers
14. Decision Making for Managers
15. Conflict Management for Managers.

Series: Financial Freedom at Any Age.

- ➢ Achieving Financial Freedom in your 20's
- ➢ Achieving Financial Freedom in your 30's
- ➢ Achieving Financial Freedom in your 40's
- ➢ Achieving Financial Freedom in your 50's
- ➢ Achieving Financial Freedom in your 60's
- ➢ Achieving Financial Freedom in your 70's and beyond.
- ➢ Achieving Financial Freedom in children
- ➢ Achieving Financial Freedom in teenagers
- ➢ Achieving Financial Freedom in college students.
- ➢ Financial Scams to be Aware of in Retirement.

Series: Personal Finance for You.
- ➢ Buying and Selling Crypto for Beginners
- ➢ Why Investing in Dividend Stocks Makes Sense.

Series: Wealth 2022.

- ➢ Online Entrepreneurship.
- ➢ Starting Your Own Business
- ➢ Wealth Management
- ➢ Passive Income.
- ➢ 12 Steps to Starting your own business.

Series: Excellent Customer Service.

- ➢ Excellent Customer Service in Retail
- ➢ Excellent Customer Service in Fast Food
- ➢ Excellent Customer Service in Full-Service Restaurant
- ➢ Excellent Customer Service in Teaching.
- ➢ Excellent Customer Service in Real Estate
- ➢ Excellent Customer Service in a Call Center
- ➢ Excellent Customer Service as a Receptionist
- ➢ Excellent Customer Service in a Hotel
- ➢ Excellent Customer Service in Selling
- ➢ Excellent Customer Service No Matter the Situation.

- Excellent Customer Service in Dental Office
- Excellent Customer Service in Medical Office.

Series: Quick Money.

- Quick Money in a Week
- Quick Money in a Weekend
- Quick Money in a Month
- Quick Money for Students.

Series: How to Promote.

- How to Make your Business Thrive During a Recession
- How to Promote your Recipe Book
- How to Promote your Children Book.

Author Bio

D.K. Hawkins. D.K. enjoys reading personal business books as well as spending time outdoors. More books will come in this collection, so please follow on Amazon for more books.

Thank you for your purchase of this book.

I honestly do appreciate it and appreciate you, my excellent customer.

God Bless You.

D.K. Hawkins.

www.ingramcontent.com/pod-product-compliance
Lightning Source LLC
Chambersburg PA
CBHW050012230526
45465CB00003BB/1386